MOBILE ADDICTION IN TODAY'S YOUTH

DHANESH GHANASHYAM GAWDE

Copyright © Dhanesh Ghanashyam Gawde
All Rights Reserved.

This book has been published with all efforts taken to make the material error-free after the consent of the author. However, the author and the publisher do not assume and hereby disclaim any liability to any party for any loss, damage, or disruption caused by errors or omissions, whether such errors or omissions result from negligence, accident, or any other cause.

While every effort has been made to avoid any mistake or omission, this publication is being sold on the condition and understanding that neither the author nor the publishers or printers would be liable in any manner to any person by reason of any mistake or omission in this publication or for any action taken or omitted to be taken or advice rendered or accepted on the basis of this work. For any defect in printing or binding the publishers will be liable only to replace the defective copy by another copy of this work then available.

Hello everyone,

I would like to dedicate this book towards my College, Shri Pancham Khemraj Mahavidhyalay (Mumbai University) and towards our Head of Commerce Department, Mr. Sachin Deshmukh sir.

I thank you sir for suggesting this wonderful subject to me.

I told my mother about it. She was excited to hear what Sir had suggested to me. My mother also helped me a lot for this big project. And I have never seen my mother so happy because I was so addicted to cell phones.

I also spend more time on mobile and less time studying.

But after writing about this topic, I realized how mobile can have side effects and gave me results also.

So once again for giving me the opportunity to write on this subject, I thank my college sir, Shri. Sachin Deshmukh sir.

And I also thank my Mother Mrs. Sonalika Ghanashyam Gawde and my Aunty Mrs. Sakhi Vivek Vichare. My Mother and my Aunty inspired me a lot and I am starting to write this book.

Thank you.

Contents

Foreword   *vii*

Summary

Introduction

Advantages Of Using Cell Phones

Disadvantages Of Using Cell Phones

Signs Of Cell Phone Addiction In Teens

Smartphone Addiction: What Does It Cause?

Checking Cell Phones First Thing In The Morning

How Much Time Do Teens Spend On Their Phones?

Why Teenagers Are Addicted To Their Phones?

Casual Phone Use Vs. Addiction

Mobile Addiction Amongst Teens

Overcoming Mobile Phone Addiction

Teen Cell Phone Addiction: How Parents Can Help?

Conclusion   43

Foreword

<u>**Author of this book:- Dhanesh Ghanashyam Gawde**</u>

He is Dhanesh Ghanashyam Gawde, age 21. He is currently studying BBI (Banking and Insurance) at Shri Pancham Khemraj College, Sawantwadi, Sindhudurg, Maharashtra. He has also done a Diploma in Computer Engineering. He also likes to read and write books, stories, shayari, quotes etc. He also often likes to write horror stories.

So far he has written 4 books which are as follows –

1) 50 Reasons to live your life,

2) Dil Se Judi 50 Shaayaris,

3) To stay or leave:- Forgiving the Unforgivable (English version and the fourth book is in Marathi Edition). These books are available on Amazon, Flipkart, Notion Press, etc. You can also read his blogs.

His Blogger ID: - Unreliable62.blogspot.com

You can also follow him on his Instagram handle.

Instagram ID: - unreliableuniform62

Thank you.

Summary

"Hello, hello! I'm talking mobile! I am your darling mobile! Why am I so happy today? I don't need to tell you how much I love you. I was happy because of this friendship. But it was also a bit sour. Everybody blamed me. I'm spoiling the kids. There were many allegations against me, such as lack of use and lack of appreciation. "It simply came to our notice then. The children would leave their studies or important work and play with me. Often I would get immersed in sports close to me. Even big men were abusing me. Chatting for hours, sending useless text messages is common. Talking with my help while walking or driving on the road has often led to serious incidents. Some people have lost their lives while crossing the road or crossing the railway tracks. Some have used me to discredit many. All of this brought me into disrepute. So I was sad. It wasn't my fault, it was the stupidity of my users. Still, I was optimistic. I believed that one day the truth would come out and prove my usefulness. Well done.

"Friends, how much use can I make? I don't need to tell you anything about Facebook. You can share all your gossip with your friends through Facebook. Many have used Facebook for business, royalty and social campaigns. Some major crimes have been uncovered by Facebook. Like Facebook, the use of websites like YouTube, Tumblr, Pin Interest, Liquin has also proved useful. Now WhatsApp application is becoming very popular.

"You can save and send your documents, photos, videos yourself. Not only that, you can make your own movie. As you send your information for the job, you can send the information by filming the statement itself.

"It simply came to our notice then because it will be too small. You know what? I will notify you immediately if money is deposited in your bank account, withdrawn from it or any transaction related to that account. Not only that, but it can help you pay anyone out of your account. It helps hotels and shops to pay their bills. But even paying for street vegetables can help me. Now your bank will be in your pocket because of me. Consider how big an impact this is going to have on the country's economy.

Mobile phones give us the liberty to connect with anyone around the world spontaneously. They empower us to find any information we require and are a great source of entertainment. While this device was designed to empower us, sadly. It's turning out to subjugate us. Almost every mobile user is suffering from the addiction of mobile these days. Everyone these days is pinned to his or her cell phone. While we may deny this as a common behavior in the present times, the truth is that it has great communicative and behavior consequences in people. This is because its effects are dangerous. Mobile addiction causes several problems such as weakened vision, headache, sleep disorders, depression, stress, aggressive behavior, social isolation, financial situations, ruined relationship and no or low professional growth. We must limit the use of mobile to take control of our lives. It might be difficult at first, but family and friends support can help overcome mobile phones addiction.

The mobile phone is one of the most significant discoveries of the 20th century. According to recent statistics, over 50 crore Indians are using smartphones. While it is true that the advancement of technology has led to many conveniences in our world, it has also brought many other critical issues to us. Mobile phone addiction is one of the instances where technology has affected people's lives adverse. With the recent burst of iPhone, Androids, and other similar smart gadgets like the tablets, the cell phone addiction issue has risen to an alarming rate.

Introduction

Mobile phones enable us to coddle in online shopping, online games, and many more. They connect us with people worldwide, we can also click pictures, watch movies, surf the internet, listen to music, and enjoy different other activities. It is difficult not to get addicted to this substation of entertainment. However, it is necessary not to fall victim to it as its consequences could be damaging. Mobile phones are designed for our convenience and our benefit. We must limit the use of mobile phones or instead it may take charge of our lives. If we feel, we are getting addicted to our mobile phones; we need to look for methods and ideas to get rid of it. We should also consider it as our duty to help our near ones, to get rid of this mobile addiction.

Mobile phone addiction is increasing by the day. People have become delusional as they have designed a new world for themselves with their mobile phones making it their pivotal component in their lives. It is deplorable to observe how mobile obsession is robbing people of their real lives.

An average Indian consumes 1,800 hours a year on his mobile phone. That is approximately one-third of his waking hours. The impact of obsession with smartphones; internet, and television is that less than 30 percent of people meet family and friends multiple times a month.

Now we will see some Advantages and Disadvantages of using mobile phones.

Advantages of Using Cell Phones

I. **Advantages of using Mobile Phones:-**

There are several good uses of mobile phones, it occupies an important place in our daily life. It has changed the lifestyle of people to an unimaginable extent. The advantages of mobile phones are enlisted as under,

a. **Keeps us connected: -** Now we can be connected to our friends, relatives at any time we want through many apps. Now we can talk video chat with whoever we want, by just operating your mobile phone or smartphone. Apart from this mobile also keeps us updated about the whole world.

a. **<u>Day to day communicating: -</u>** Today mobile phones has made our life so easy for daily life activities. Today, one can assess the live traffic situation on mobile phone and take appropriate decisions to reach on time. Along with it the weather updates, booking a cab and many more.

c. **<u>Entertainment for all: -</u>** With the improvement of mobile technology, the whole entertainment world is now under one roof. Whenever we get bored with routine work or during the breaks, we can listen to music, watch movies, our favorite shows or just watch the video of one's favorite song.

d. **<u>Managing office work: -</u>** These days' mobiles are used for many types of official work from meeting schedules, sending and receiving documents, giving presentations, alarms, job applications, etc. Mobile phones have become an essential device for every working people.

e. **<u>Mobile Banking: -</u>** Nowadays mobiles are even used as a wallet for making payments. Money could be transferred almost instantly to friends, relatives or others by using mobile banking in the smartphones. Also, one can easily access his/her account details and know past transactions. So it saves a lot of time and also hassle-free.

f. One can play games an order to get fresh and use mind. Smart phones provide many online and offline games. One can pass free time playing games.

g. There are several useful apps which helps us a lot. Informative, educational apps help students to learn being at home.

h. Mobile phones are a miracle in the life of students, they can search information about different topics using net in their mobile phones.

i. During Journey or on any trip one can capture pictures in their smart phones and can save unlimited pictures in their smart phones.

j. One can install useful apps in smartphones like Microsoft Word and
    Excel apps for writing diary and writing poetry and articles.

Disadvantages of Using Cell Phones

I. **<u>Disadvantages of Mobile Phones: -</u>**

a. **<u>Wasting Time: -</u>** Nowadays people have become addicted to mobiles. Even when we don't need to mobile we surf the net, play games making a real addict. As mobile phones became smarter, people became dumber.

a. **<u>Making us non-communicable: -</u>** Wide usage of mobiles has resulted in less meet and talk more. Now people don't meet physically rather chat or comment on social media.

c. **<u>Loss of privacy: -</u>** It is a major concern now of losing one's privacy because of much mobile usage. Today anyone could easily access the information like where you live, your friends and family, what is your occupation, where is your house, etc.; by just easily browsing through your social media account.

d. **Money wastage:** - As the usefulness of mobiles has increased so their costing. Today people are spending a lot amount of money on buying smartphones, which could rather be spent on more useful things like education, or other useful things in our life.

e. Students waste their precious time playing online games in their smartphones. Instead of studying they either play games or spend their time watching movies and clips.

f. It is used as a sophisticated weapon by terrorists and criminals. Most of the plans of killing are communicated using mobile phone, thousands of precious lives are lost due to mobile phones.

g. Children start watching porn videos and inappropriate content using mobile phone which destroys their moral and ethical standing in the society.

h. It destroy the health, especially students use mobile phones till the late hours of night, they do not sleep appropriately and it is dangerous to use mobile at night, it affects eyesight and leaves negative impacts on the psychology of a person. Unnecessary night awakening has become common due to mobile phones.

i. Telling lies and deceiving others has become common among people. Love affairs, deceptions and betrayal are the product of mobile phones. Young boys and girls hurt each other's feelings through mobile phones.

j. Students use it for cheating during exams, they ignore their studies and start relying on cheating.

Signs of Cell Phone Addiction in Teens

As a parent or guardian, the easiest way to help your teen deal with cell phone addiction is by understanding the signs and symptoms. These will be indicators that your kid is being controlled by mobile tech. force and needs your help.

Cell Phone Addiction in Teens

Here are some of the signs to look out for:-

1). <u>Teen Spending Hours On Their Cell Phone:-</u>

If you observe that your child or ward is spending hours on their cell phone, there's a chance they're battling with a concept known as "Tolerance."

It means the insatiable quest to reach a desired high. This is similar to alcohol or drug abuse.

This has become a norm in our day — since millions of people are now using cell phones, coupled with increased downloads that make the next shiny app or platform a click away. Even students aren't left behind...

60% of college students say they're addicted to their cell phones.

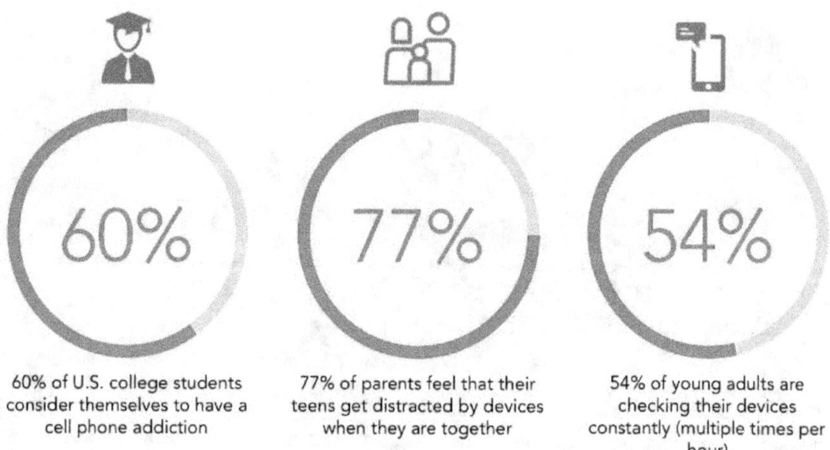

<u>Addiction Percentage</u>

If the only thing a teen does at leisure or while hanging out with friends is to use their cell phones, there's a risk of addiction.

2). <u>Teen Becoming Agitated When Their Cell Phone is Misplaced:-</u>

How does your teen react when they misplace their cell phone. Of course, they have to be concerned, but getting all-worked up over a mobile device can be a sign of an addiction. A recent study shows that 68% of older teenagers are afraid of losing their phone.

<u>Reactions</u>

As a mom, dad, or guardian, you might notice some withdrawal symptoms such as irritability, desperation, panic, stress, and even anxiety in your teen — when they're separated from their cell phone.

It doesn't matter how long or whether they end up losing the phone, does it hinder their normal life in any way?

3). <u>**Complaints from People Over a Teen's Phone Use:-**</u>

Another sign of cell phone addiction in a teen is when people (friends, relatives, colleagues, or even acquaintances have complained about your child's phone use.

You have to take this 'sign' with a grain of salt because not all complaints are true — but when it's from people who you respect and value their opinions, you shouldn't pay a deaf ear to their complaints. "

Conscious use of phones while driving, riding a bike, or in prohibited context should be avoided," says Justin Baker.

<u>Conflicts</u>

This can result in an outcome known as "Conflict" which is common in cell phone addiction issues.

It may not even come as a complaint. If your teenager lets cell phone beeps or notification sound interfere with their social engagements or vacation time, it could be a source of concern.

4). <u>Switching Between Multiple Devices and Applications:-</u>

This sign is an obvious indicator of some form of teen cell phone addiction.

Switching between multiple applications and multitasking at the same time is popular with teens because smartphones have several features that allow that.

Modern phones even allow users to share screen — so that they can use 3 to 4 platforms or applications at the same time.

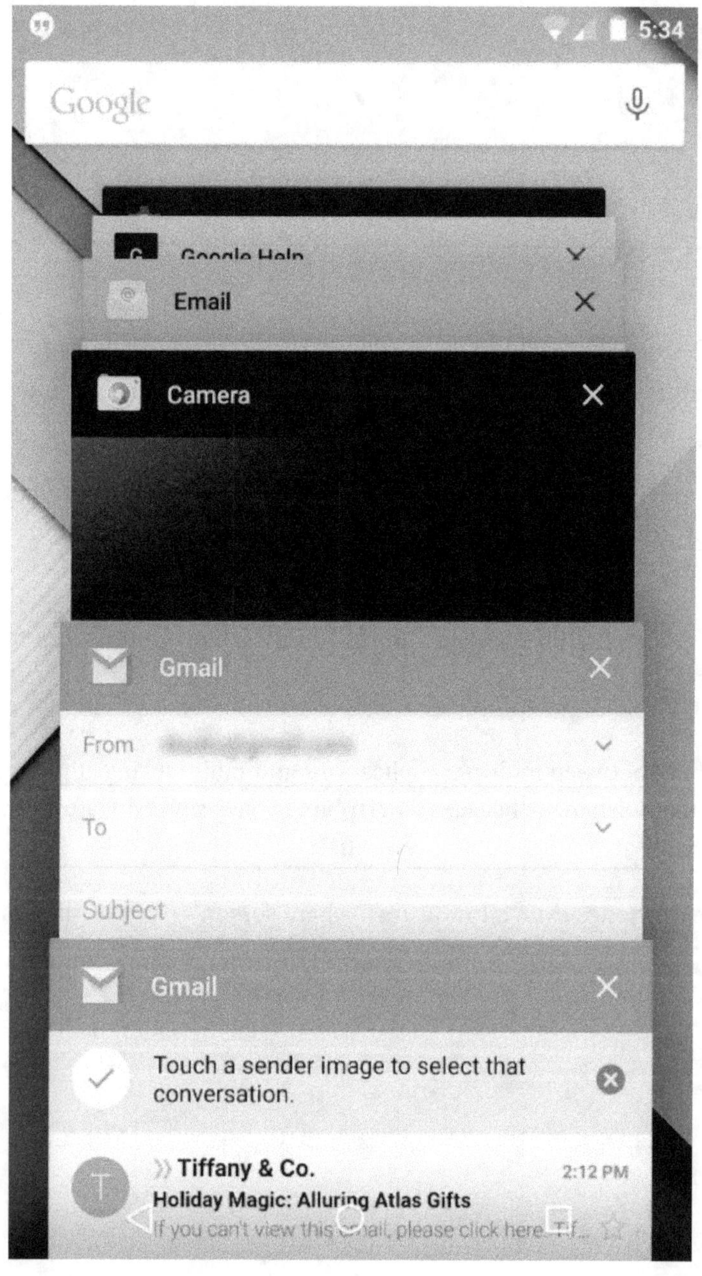

Switching Between Multiple Devices

Some teenagers can't do one thing at a given time on their cell phones. They'd rather prefer to use social media, or texting their friends, or playing a new game on the go.

This creates a loop that keeps them stuck.

5). <u>Inability to Put Away the Cell Phone:-</u>

Most teenagers struggle to put away their cell phone for a few hours. This can cause a situation popularly referred to as "Relapse."

It occurs when a teen is determined to cut back on cell phone use but finds him or herself being controlled by a strong force that forces them to reach for the phone.

Relapse is common with people undergoing therapy or treatment associated with drug abuse. But it happens to teens who are addicted to their cell phones.

An average of 80% of recovering addicts experiences at least one mild relapse, according to Psychology Today.

Recovering Addicts

Since most teenagers haven't developed their mental capacities, it can be a struggle to consciously create new habits or resist the urge to reach for their cell phones.

New habits such as reach a hardcopy book or playing outdoors with friends can help the teen practice being "unplugged" for a few hours each day.

If a teen has been self-diagnosed with cell phone addiction, half the battle of getting the right solution is already won.

There's no need to give up on cell phone use entirely, but there should be times when your kid should stay away from their phones and create new habits and develop new skills.

To help your teenager, you can turn off the phone and leave it in the car or the study. As much as possible, the cell phone should be out of reach for your kid. You may also want to adopt a nighttime charging practice in any room, but definitely not the bedroom.

Help your teenager to create a new lifestyle and enjoy life without relying on a cell phone. After all, there was life before the cell phone and there will be life, even after the cell phone is gone (will it ever be gone?).

Smartphone Addiction: What does it Cause?

Smartphone addiction is a concept that examines the fear of not keeping up with the happenings on the internet or cellular service. It happens in both teens and adults, but more pronounced in the former because of the stage they're in.

Smartphones

Several studies have shown a correlation between mental health issues and smartphone addiction. But correlation doesn't necessarily mean causation.

Therefore, even though it's popularly known that phone addiction leads to loneliness, anxiety, and depression, the major concern is whether or not these symptoms are primarily caused by addiction.

Here's another school of thought:

Are people with anxiety, depression, and other vices more prone to become dependent on their smartphones?

In new research that was conducted by the University of Arizona to understand the connecting line between mental health and smartphone use, a group of 18 to 20-year-olds took part in it.

These participants are regarded as "older adolescents" by researchers — and they are among the first to have witnessed the transformative power of smart technology (the first iPhone was released in 2007).

"Dependence" was the major focus of the study. The researchers examined a person's psychological reliance on a smartphone, not general usage.

Participants answered questions such as "I panic when I can't use my phone," in addiction to other questions related to depression and loneliness using a four-point scale.

Addiction is a chronic disease and is one of the most intractable health disorders faced around the world. Mobile addiction is a thriving concern. It is very easy to get addicted to cell phones but difficult to subdue them. A lot of people globally are addicted to their mobile phones. The mobile addict's behavior pattern is more or less the same as the others. Here are some certain signs and symptoms that clearly show that a person is addicted to his/her mobile phone.

Nearly everyone worldwide has a cellphone, so how can we tell if someone is experiencing mobile phone addiction syndrome from someone who is not?

Like most diseases and illness, one can deduce if someone is undergo the exhibited symptoms syndrome. Research has revealed that using mobile phones have killed 6,000 people each year. Besides that, here are some other effects of cell phone addiction that can affect us.

1. **<u>Back and Neck problem:-</u>**

This is a common problem that all phone addicts deal with. Most people arched down when they used their phones looking down at the mobile phone for an extended period causes them to have back and neck pain issues. According to studies, 45% of the youngsters from the age of 16 to 24 years suffer from back pain due to the over usage of mobile phones. Besides that, the endless swapping of phones and texting can make our fingers stiff.

1. **<u>Stress, Anxiety, and Depression:-</u>**

Another common effect that we usually hear from experts is mental and emotional health problems. When we spend too much time on our phones, we neglect other elements of our life, and as a result, our life gets out of balance. Staring the mobile screen for too long can also make us feel anxious and stressed.

3. **<u>Health Issue:-</u>**

Spending too much time with our mobile phone can also give us less time to exercise or even walk around. Mobile phones usage has considerably displaced many of our physical activities in life. A poll conducted on a group of school children found that those who employ long hours using their phones were less fit than those who spent less time on their phones.

In the end, the researchers deduced that indeed, smartphone addiction is a predictor for anxious and depressive symptoms.

Checking Cell Phones First Thing in the Morning

A lot of teenagers check their mobile phones first thing in the morning. 46% do it before getting out of bed, while 80% do so without brushing their teeth. It's funny but true!

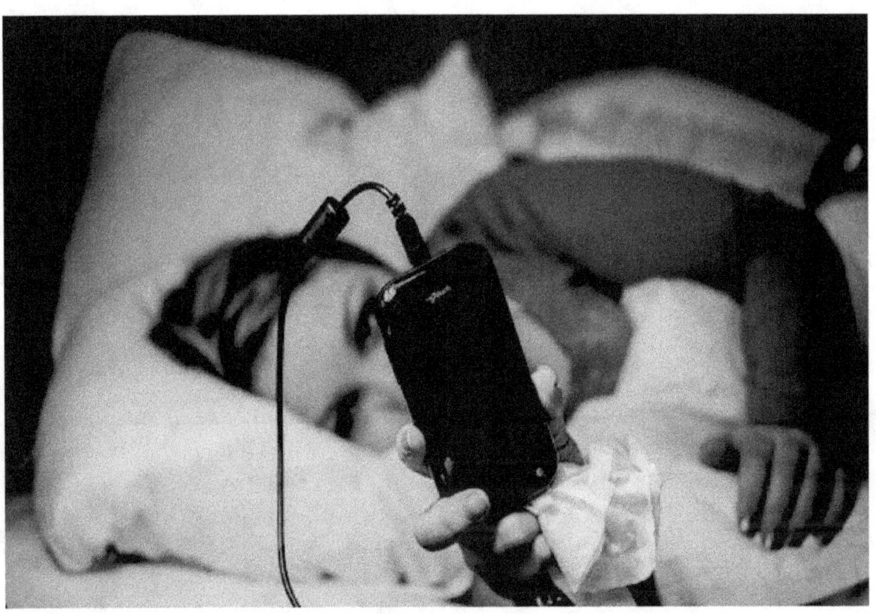

Checking Cellphones

For teenagers, when this becomes a daily routine, it can negatively affect their sleep — because the human brain is wired to respond to stimuli that we've developed over a long time. The brain can pick the signals and translate them as being natural.

This behavior is known as Salience, which can be integrated into the human brain.

In some cases, routinely checking cell phones can dominate their thinking and emotions. This would cause them to sleep with their phones next to their beds.

A quick way to help your teen is to keep the phone out of reach, until they're fully awake and ready for the day.

How Much Time Do Teens Spend on Their Phones?

Teens Spend on Phones

According to statistics, teenagers spends an average of 6.3 hours staring at their cell phone screen.

This is similar to the same amount of time an average adult spends working. 6 hours is huge and it could leave serious debris on the body and mind.

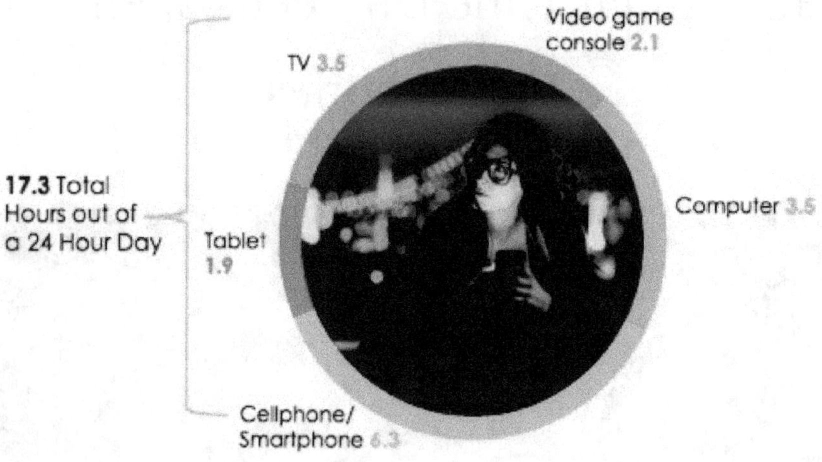

Time Spend on Gadgets

Cell phone addicted teens exhibit several signs of mental health issues. Anxiety and depression are both common occurrences in teens.

Given the misinformation on social media (which comes from excessive use of the internet-enabled cell phone), we're experiencing a rise in teen suicide rates. The societal dependence on mobile phones has caused a lot of havoc than good.

You may not fully understand the extent to which a teen is addicted to their cell phone, but just observe their behavior when they hear the sound of a notification alert on their cell phone.

For some teens, it can be very difficult to resist but impossible for most of the teens that are battling with phone addiction. I guess this is one of the signs you should look out for in your teen.

Most teens spend free time on their phones while others use theirs to learn new things or connect with friends.

Truly, Smartphones can be very useful to teens especially for online research and casual use on social media.

Why Teenagers Are Addicted to their Phones?

The truth be told, teens and technology are like two Siamese twins that can't be separated.

Parents shouldn't attempt to completely prevent their kids from using smartphones – preventing addiction is the pursuit — since it's already causing family conflicts, according to a survey conducted for Common Sense Media.

Is It Causing Family Conflicts?

Teens and parents say they argue about device use:

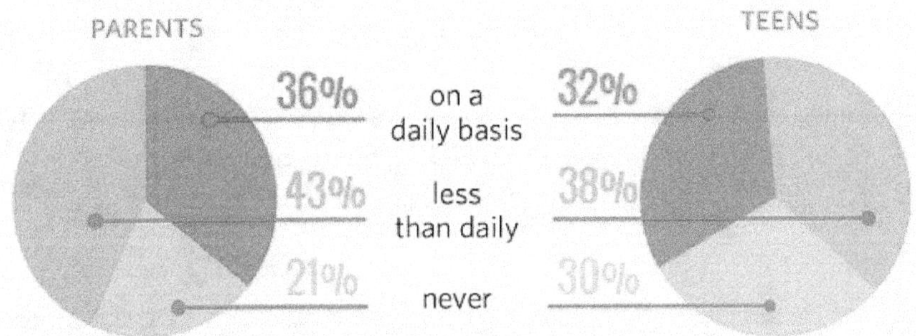

<u>Family Conflicts</u>

Teens use technology in the classroom to improve their grades.

They also connect and meet new friends on social media through various platforms and apps. And with so many tasks to do every day, teens use apps to stay organized and productivity (in most cases).

There's so much pressure in today's mobile-first environment. Cell phone use has become a necessity — teens can't do without it. Even recreational activities that are designed to help teens relieve stress are all attached to mobile phones.

As parents, there's a responsibility to ensure that our kids use their phones to keep up with their busy lives and learn, but it shouldn't result in more stress. Parents can help teenagers navigate the stressful and distracting world of technology.

Casual Phone Use Vs. Addiction

How does casual use of cell phones differ from addiction? How can parents determine what the teen's apparent obsession with a smartphone becomes an addictive behavior?

I'm sure you know how difficult it can be to attempt to communicate with a teen who can't put away their cell phone?

Given that teens use their smartphones for both productive and unhealthy ways, including for academic research and personal use (often at the same time), a good way to draw the line is by understanding how they use their smartphones and less on how long they use it.

It's all about striking a balance between the amount of time and how teenagers use their cell phones and what objective that use serves them.

For example, teenagers can use YouTube to learn new topics as well as watch funny videos (i.e., academic and personal uses).

Truly, distinguishing between normal daily cell phone use and addicted use is important. Since the rule isn't set on a stone, here are some of the questions you need to ask — it'll shine a brighter light on that thin line:

- Does my teen neglect social events to be with their phone instead?
- Is my teen's relationship with siblings, friends, or school work negatively impacted by smartphone use?
- What major eating and sleeping behaviors are obvious in my teen?
- Does my teen get irritated or even violent when the phone is withdrawn from them?

Note: These are not the only questions or signs to look out in your teen. Every parent knows their child, so it's easy to study their behaviors — especially when it comes to cell phone use.

Mobile addiction amongst teens

A mobile phone serves as an escapism from the obstacles and problems of practical life. People of every age group undergo mobile addiction. Nonetheless, teenagers are most prone to acquire this addiction. Teenagers are in that stage of their life where they are learning and traversing new things. They have various questions, and their mobile phones have almost all their answers. Children these days have a lot of things to ask and share but are often reluctant to discuss or speak about the same with their teachers or parents.

Most parents these days are so engaged in their work that they don't have the time to speak or monitor their kids. And secondly, there are many things where they get embarrassed to ask, and for this reason, the mobile phone becomes their source of guidance. They also make friends online and adequately share their feelings with them.

Teens addicted to mobile phones are very dangerous. They cannot focus on their studies, as this addiction hinders their capability to focus and reduces their ability to understand things. Those addicted to mobile phones also have a greater chance of acquiring habits such as drinking, smoking, and taking drugs. They also become socially incompetent as they are always on their mobile phone. Therefore their future remains at stake. Parents must make sure that they do not give smartphones to their teenage kids. Teens need to focus on their education and traverse their interest in different beneficial activities. They should adequately explore the world and not by wasting their valuable time on a mobile phone.

Overcoming mobile phone addiction

With other types of obsessions or addictions, one cannot overwhelm mobile addiction unless they do not want to give up on it sincerely. The obsession of mobile phones is one of the consequences on how technology has affected people's lives.

Once, you are determined, to get over mobile addicted, we can do so by following the below-mentioned tips:-

By limiting the use of the mobile phone and setting the number of hours, we aim to consume on our mobile each day and assigning a fixed amount of time for each activity such as texting, social media, gaming or watching videos will help us to overcome the addiction of mobile phones.

We can also get engaged in dancing, painting, playing indoor and outdoor games, doing household chores, reading books, and many other activities. This will reduce our urge to check our mobile phone constantly. Spending time with our parents, helping our spouse with work, indulging in different fun activities or going out to new places an also help you to get rid of this addiction.

If the addiction of mobiles becomes to solicit professional guidance. Many therapists specialize in mobile addiction therapy, and they offer individual and group therapy to help get rid of this addiction.

Teen Cell Phone Addiction: How Parents Can Help?

In this section, we'll discover the right steps that parents can take to help a teen who's addicted to their mobile phone.

Bear in mind that these 'tips' may not provide an overnight result — parents must keep at, encourage their teens to develop strong will and control and make them see reasons why they should never be addicted to anything — drug, games, movies, phone, etc.

Let's dive in.

1. <u>Educate Your Teen:-</u>

Given the importance of a mobile phone; communicating with your teen and help them explore the world for good, you need to give your teen the best device that will serve them well.

Educate your Teen

But there's a need for education. Teach them how to use the phone in a good way; while unveiling the dangers of modern technology. Make sure you set boundaries and do everything with love — so that your teen knows it's for their good.

While educating your teen, you should adopt some degree of monitoring. That way, you'll keep a close tab on your teen when they're not with you.

Getting addicted to a smartphone is easy. Before giving your teen control, provide tools and let them know they can always ask questions.

2. Provide a Structure:-

Teenagers want to be loved and feel they're a part of something big. So you need to provide a structure when giving your child a phone.

Be clear on what you want them to do with the cell phone, how often they should use it, and even challenge them to make better use of it for a prize.

Set a framework of expectation that will persuade your teen to stick to a consistent routine. This is a great way to support young people and get the best from them.

As a parent, there should be a culture in your home. The use of cell phones must be incorporated into this system of culture — as your teen grows, they'll come to terms with it. After all, it's a structure that 'mom' says to follow.

3. Set Boundaries for PhoneUse:-

In addition to providing a structure in your home, you also need to be clear on what to do in certain areas around the home.

For example, should teens use phones while eating? Of course, that's a no-no!

So when you're on a family outing, attending social events, at the dining table, or studying, these times and places aren't good for teens to use their cell phones. Relationships come first and must be respected.

4. <u>Set a Good Example:-</u>

As a parent, you can't possibly attempt to help your teen with cell phone addiction if you're always glued to your phone. You don't want kids to learn inappropriate behavior concerning phone use in the home.

<u>Good Example</u>

If you've set a structure or established screen-free zones, you have to obey it. Because teens, most of the time, learn from their parents. They learn from observation!

5. <u>**Create a Policy:-**</u>

When should your teen(s) use their cell phones and laptops? Well, there's never a standard time but when they're in bed, they shouldn't use it.

Because bright screens can negatively affect sleep, which, in turn, could lead to insomnia.

It's wise to create a plan that will help your teens to check cell phones and laptops — it could be in the evening and after 8:00 a.m. Blue lights from cell phones can harm sleep, so keep them away.

<u>**Blue Light**</u>

Conclusion

Mobile is an essential part of our lives. It has a lot of advantages along with disadvantages. Its essence is instant connectivity for the good of mankind. They are convenient, easily accessible, and of great use. All, one has to remember, is that mobiles are invented for our convenience and not to create a nuisance. If used judiciously, wisely and with public etiquette, mobiles can be of great use. A mobile phone could both be positive or negative; depending how a user uses it. As mobiles have become a part of our life so we should use it in a proper way, carefully for our better hassle-free life rather using it improperly and making it a virus in life.

Mobile addiction can destroy our life if it is not stopped on time. As much as we ignore it, mobile addiction has grown into a big problem today. It is hindering our professional life and personal relations. Mobile phones are creating more impairment than being beneficial. People undergoing this mobile addiction problem must try to get rid of it and revert to the real world. Getting rid of this addiction might be challenging, but it is not impossible. With the support from the loved ones and some effort from oneself, we can overcome this problem over time, and if that does not help, we shouldn't hesitate to solicit professional advice.

If you feel or notice signs of phone addiction in your teen, you should implement the tips above to help them curb the negative effects.

You may also want to speak to a mental healthcare provider for advice on how to help your teen learn healthy habits so they can take control of their life and overcome every cell phone addiction. Because they can do it!

There are different rehabilitation options available for cell phone addicted teens — a quick search online will show you a nearby center.

www.ingramcontent.com/pod-product-compliance
Lightning Source LLC
Chambersburg PA
CBHW061726130726
47996CB00006B/2518